Managing Projects

2O MINUTE MANAGER SERIES

Get up to speed fast on essential business skills. Whether you're looking for a crash course or a brief refresher, you'll find just what you need in HBR's 20-Minute Manager series—foundational reading for ambitious professionals and aspiring executives. Each book is a concise, practical primer, so you'll have time to brush up on a variety of key management topics.

Advice you can quickly read and apply, from the most trusted source in business.

Titles include:

Creating Business Plans

Delegating Work

Finance Basics

Managing Projects

Managing Time

Managing Up

Presentations

Running Meetings

2O MINUTE MANAGER SERIES

Managing Projects

Create your schedule
Monitor your budget
Meet your goals

HARVARD BUSINESS REVIEW PRESS

Boston, Massachusetts

The web addresses referenced in this book were live and correct at
the time of the book's publication but may be subject to change.

Library of Congress Cataloging-in-Publication Data

Managing projects.
    pages cm. — (20-minute manager series)
  ISBN 978-1-62527-083-2 (alk. paper)
  1. Project management.
  HD69.P75M3634 2014
  658.4'04—dc23

                            2013039031

ISBN: 9781625270832
eISBN: 9781625270887

Preview

You've been asked to manage a project. Or you know you soon will be.

No surprise there, since every business involves a lot of projects. If you're a leader—or if you hope to become one—then "project manager" will eventually be part of your job description.

But don't worry. You're starting with the right book. Here you'll get a brief, useful tour of what's involved in:

- Defining a project.

- Setting clear goals and milestones.

- Putting together a terrific team.

- Scheduling and monitoring key tasks.

- Keeping stakeholders in the loop.

- Dealing with problems like scope creep and cost overruns.

- Bringing your project to a successful close.

Contents

Contents

Contents

Managing Projects

The Basics

The Basics

To begin, let's talk about what a project is and what project management is all about. As you'll see, every project can be broken down into four phases—planning, build-up, implementation, and closeout—which makes the whole enterprise a lot easier to get your mind around. You're likely to encounter bumps along the way, so we'll also touch on how to handle the most common problems.

What constitutes a project

A project is a good-sized task that someone wants done. Unlike a **process**, it has a beginning, middle, and end.

Building a house is a project. So is launching a new product or developing a new marketing campaign.

Some companies are project-based—that's all they do. Think of construction and engineering firms, custom manufacturers, advertising agencies, and so on. Other businesses rely on processes for their everyday operations, launching a project only when they want to make a change or undertake something new. For example, a health-care center might sponsor a project to redesign its patient-intake procedures.

Whatever the context, the word **project** usually refers to a well-defined task involving a group of people working together. Projects can last any amount of time, but most take somewhere between a month and a year to complete.

What project management involves

Every project needs someone in charge. Big projects, such as constructing a power plant, are led by professional project managers. Smaller ones, such as creating a marketing brochure for a new pharmaceutical, tend to be run by people who must add the project to their regular work.

Regardless of job size, the buck stops with these project managers. They must see the project through from start to finish. They draw up the plan, assemble the team, decide how to allocate resources, schedule the work, watch the budget, solve problems, and do a lot of other things as well. It can be a big responsibility, even when the project is modest in scope.

What's more, project managers often find themselves working with a team of volunteers—colleagues who have regular assignments and supervisors but who have agreed to contribute time to the project. When that's the case, the project managers rarely have direct authority over their team members, so they must get people working together effectively without giving orders.

In short, project management requires organizational skills, financial skills, and people skills.

Fortunately, you can learn all these skills through study and experience. This book will help you get started.

The four phases of every project

What do designing a car, developing a website, moving a company, cleaning up a disaster site, and updating an information system have in common? They're all projects, and they all go through the same four phases:

- *Planning.* In this initial phase, you define the problem and identify the **stakeholders**—that is, everybody who has a vested interest in the project. You also map out your goals and determine what you'll need to accomplish them.

- *Build-up.* This is when you assemble your team, plan the individual tasks, develop a schedule and a budget, and hold your kickoff meeting.

- *Implementation.* Now the project is underway. People are busy working on their assigned tasks. You're holding regular meetings, monitoring the schedule and the budget, and preparing regular reports. Oh, yes—you're also resolving the many unexpected issues that inevitably pop up.

- *Closeout.* The project is complete. Your job is to hand it off to whoever will be responsible for the final product or the new process. You review the team's accomplishments and "lessons learned," and you prepare a final report.

Each phase has its own set of goals, activities, tools, and skills. As a project manager, you'll articulate the goals, prepare your team to carry out the activities, and use each set of tools and skills as needed (see table 1).

Even though each phase is different, you'll find yourself returning to tasks from earlier phases. For

TABLE 1

Project phases

Planning	Build-up	Implementation	Closeout
ACTIVITIES			
Determine the real problem to solve	Assemble your team	Monitor and control process and budget	Evaluate project performance
Identify stakeholders	Plan assignments	Report progress	Close the project
Define project objectives	Create the schedule	Hold weekly team meetings	Debrief with the team
Determine scope, resources, and major tasks	Hold a kickoff meeting	Manage problems	Develop a post-evaluation report
Prepare for trade-offs	Develop a budget		
KEY SKILLS			
Task analysis	Process analysis	Supervising	Follow-through
Planning	Team building	Leading and motivating	Planning
Cost-benefit analysis of options	Delegating	Communication	Communication
	Negotiating	Conflict management	
	Recruiting and hiring	Problem solving	
	Communication		
TOOLS			
Work Breakdown Structure	Scheduling tools (CPM, PERT, Gantt)		Post-evaluation report: analysis and lessons learned

example, you typically begin the planning phase with a ballpark figure for your budget and an estimated completion date for the project. Once you're in the build-up phase, you begin to define the details of the project plan. These details give you new information, so you revise the budget and schedule accordingly. This doesn't mean you're moving backward. You're just incorporating what you've learned into the overall plan. You're seeing more of the big picture with each step you take.

Planning Your Project

Planning Your Project

T he first phase in managing a project is to make an overall plan. Usually this involves just five steps:

1. Define the real problem.

2. Identify your stakeholders.

3. Set the project's goals.

4. Prepare for trade-offs.

5. Spell out the tasks.

We'll look at each one in turn.

Define the real problem

Too often, project managers leap to the solution before they completely understand what they are trying to solve. As a result, they miss the mark and disappoint their stakeholders. That's why defining the problem is such a critical step.

Imagine you're an IT manager, for example, and you've been asked to lead a team developing a new database and data entry system. It would be tempting to jump right in, relying on your own assumptions about what the system should include. But will that solve your company's problem? First you'll want to find out what your supervisors are trying to fix. Maybe they can't get data out of the system fast enough. Maybe they can't find all the information they require in one place. Before designing the new system, you need to know what outputs people are looking for, how they will use these outputs, how soon they must have the redesign, and so on.

Unless you understand the underlying problem, you risk designing a solution that doesn't do what users need—or one that does far more than required. Either way, you're wasting time and money.

To focus your efforts, answer these questions:

- What issue do people think this project will address?

- Why do they see this as a problem that needs solving?

- Who has a stake in the solution or outcome?

- Do all stakeholders have the same goal, or do their goals differ?

- What criteria will people use to judge this project's success?

THE WRONG TOOL FOR THE JOB

Sometimes a project request is just wrongheaded, as in the following fictional scenario:

When Eun's boss sees the slump in quarterly revenues, he reacts immediately: "We need a new incentive plan ASAP!" He always talks like that, wanting things "ASAP" and "last week." He asks Eun to launch a project to develop the plan.

As an up-and-coming HR manager for a mid-sized hotel chain, Eun is excited to lead her first companywide project. But she knows that incentives aren't the problem. Most employees want to do a good job and serve customers well, but the hotels' processes and systems keep getting in the way. The company never puts enough time into training new recruits, and it shows. There are also problems with the registration system.

How can Eun tell her boss that a new incentive plan isn't the answer? She doesn't want to question the project's merits because this is a big opportunity for her—but she doesn't want to set herself up to fail.

Eun must help her boss clarify the project's goals. Given his ready-fire-aim style, she'll have to act quickly. For example, she might say to him, *"I'm assuming that at the end of this project, what you really want is a strategy for increasing revenue. Is that right?"* Once he agrees on the desired outcome, Eun can investigate what's causing the problem. Perhaps the registration and checkout system is cumbersome and generates customer complaints even when used properly. Perhaps the finance office reports an increased number of uncollectible bills stemming from inaccurate data entry.

Eun can then bring those problems to her boss's attention before anybody invests time and money in an ill-conceived project. She might even propose a new project to address one of the real issues.

Identify your stakeholders

Your boss, other managers, customers, team members, the finance department—all these individuals or groups can be stakeholders. They're the ones who will ultimately judge the project's success or failure.

To identify your stakeholders, answer these questions:

- Which functions or people will the project's activities or outcomes affect?

- Who will contribute resources—people, space, time, tools, and money—to the project?

- Who will use and benefit from the project's output?

Then have your stakeholders sign off on what they expect from the project and what resources they'll provide. Because stakeholders' interests vary, their definitions of success are likely to differ. You'll need to meld their expectations into a coherent, manageable set of goals.

The list of stakeholders can change in the middle of a project. A regulator or a new customer representative may show up. An executive in another unit may learn of the project and have ideas of her own about what it should accomplish. If so, respond to her requests and concerns—but include all other stakeholders in any decision to redirect the project.

Whether you're managing a project in a corporation or working as an independent consultant for a client, it's essential to have the support of the people you answer to. Though every stakeholder matters, the person who assigned or hired you to be project manager is typically the first among equals.

Clients and internal project sponsors (or their bosses) sometimes have an unrealistic view of what can be accomplished, by when, and for how much.

Usually, a little negotiating will help bring their requirements in line with the available resources. In some organizations, however, setting unrealistic goals seems to be standard operating procedure. A project manager who repeatedly faces this situation must eventually decide whether it's worth the effort. There's always a point at which you should cut your losses and get out—decline the assignment, ask to be transferred to another area of the company, or even look for another job. It's important to feel confident that the project you are embarking on has a reasonable chance of success.

Set the project's goals

Any project's success is determined by how well it meets its goals. The more explicitly you state them at the outset, the less people will disagree at the end about whether you have met them. In the planning phase, however, much is still in flux. Be prepared to revise your goals as you gather more information about what you need to achieve.

In defining goals, think SMART. They should be:

- **S**pecific

- **M**easurable

- **A**ction-oriented

- **R**ealistic

- **T**ime-limited

Here's an example:

Over the next four months, the health-care benefits task force of United Products' HR department will come up with a new benefits plan. Its SMART goals are:

1. Identify and survey (*action-oriented*) at least six (*measurable*) providers that meet the department's minimum criteria for service quality.

2. Recommend (*action-oriented*), at the June board of directors' meeting (*time-limited*), the three (*specific*) providers that offer the best and broadest coverage at a cost that is at least 10% (*realistic*) less than the company's current per-employee contribution.

Keep in mind the following factors as you set your goals:

- *Quality.* Establish the project's quality standards and determine how to measure and satisfy them.

- *Organization.* Make sure you have access to the people you need. Ultimately, your team must help you achieve your goals.

- *Communication.* Determine with your stakeholders what information they need and how best to deliver it. (Keeping stakeholders informed is *always* important.)

- *Risk.* Identify the most likely risks and evaluate possible responses.

Once you have sketched out your goals, discuss them with the person who asked you to undertake the project. Don't shrink from agreeing to ambitious goals. Just make sure you'll get the time, people, and money necessary to reach those goals.

The success of the initiative is quantified with measurable goals. In those goals, I highlight the ways in which [the support of] executive management is required for success of the project. If there isn't executive sponsorship, there are times when we won't take the job.

—**Beth Chapman, engagement manager**

Prepare for trade-offs

Scope, schedule, and budget are the three related variables that most often determine what you can achieve. The basic formula is:

Scope = Schedule + Budget

If you change one of these variables, you'll have to change at least one of the others. For instance, say your time frame for developing a new database management system is suddenly cut in half. Now you must either employ a lot more people (increasing the budget) or deliver a system with fewer features than planned (reducing the scope).

Most trade-offs aren't so dramatic; they happen frequently in the ordinary course of a project. In software projects, lead designers usually work directly with end users to discuss functionality, budget, and time lines. In construction, architects and engineers meet regularly with customers to discuss possible new features and their implications for the schedule and the budget. Remember that a less ambitious or even lower-quality product is not necessarily a bad thing. The key is to establish a level of quality or functionality that meets the needs of the end users and fits the budget and scheduling requirements. Knowing from the start which of these three variables is most important to each stakeholder will help you make appropriate trade-offs.

It's give-and-take. Everybody understands budgeting. They will be willing to give up functionality in exchange for a reduced budget or speedier delivery. They have a feel for what they have to sacrifice to get something else. Wishful thinking should be suppressed.

—Susanna Erlikh, software development project manager

Often, you will spot trade-offs long before your stakeholders do. When that happens, it's your responsibility to inform them of any changes you'd like to make in the project's scope, schedule, or budget, and then to negotiate a satisfactory solution.

Spell out the tasks

Many projects fail. They don't get the hoped-for results, or they come in way over budget or way past deadline. Often the roots of failure lie in the planning stage; the project manager overlooked a significant part of the necessary work, for example, or grossly underestimated the time and money required. One tool that can help you avoid such unfortunate outcomes is a Work Breakdown Structure, or WBS (see figure 1).

FIGURE 1

Work Breakdown Structure

Sample Planning Document

Develop a Work Breakdown Structure (WBS) to ensure that you do not overlook a significant part of a complex activity or underestimate the time and money needed to complete the work. Use multiple pages as needed.

DESCRIBE THE OVERALL PROJECT:

The overall project will migrate 3 web servers and 2 databases to a new physical data center. The project requires that 5 new servers be provisioned in the new data center: these servers will mirror the production servers existing in the old data center. The new servers will be built to the same specifications as the old ones; they will run the same applications and have the same content. Once implemented, the new equipment will be tested to confirm functionality. The sites will have a cutover and "go live" date. Finally, the old equipment will be decommissioned and reabsorbed into inventory.

MAJOR TASK

Obtain equipment.

Level 1 Subtasks

Purchase 3 web servers and 2 databases.

Ship equipment to new data center.

(continued)

Level 2 Subtasks

Cut P.O. and order servers.

Alert data center that equipment is slated for arrival.

Subtask Duration

7 days

MAJOR TASK

Provision and implement equipment.

Level 1 Subtasks

Physically install hardware.

Load operating systems.

Load applications.

Mirror content to new servers.

Level 2 Subtasks

Rack and cable new equipment in data center and ensure physical and network connectivity.

Load base-level operating systems for web and database servers.

Load application-level software, including web server software, database applications, and any required dependencies.

Copy configurations from production sites, transfer to new servers, and load appropriately.

Subtask Duration

8 days

MAJOR TASK

Test equipment.

Level 1 Subtasks
Test machines.

Level 2 Subtasks
Ensure network connectivity, as well as web and database access functionality and integrity.

Subtask Duration
2 days

MAJOR TASK

Go live with new equipment.

Level 1 Subtasks
Cut over to new production site.

Check data and content integrity.

Level 2 Subtasks
Switch web and database access to new sites.

Run a series of predetermined tests to ensure that data is accurate and that any updates since mirroring have been captured and applied as necessary.

Subtask Duration
2 days

(continued)

MAJOR TASK

Test again.

Level 1 Subtasks

Let sites burn in for 24 hours and check integrity once again.

Level 2 Subtasks

Run series of tests once more to ensure that updates and logging are functioning correctly.

Subtask Duration

1 day

MAJOR TASK

Decommission old equipment.

Level 1 Subtasks

Remove equipment from data center.

Reabsorb equipment for future use.

Level 2 Subtasks

De-install equipment; erase software and content.

Ship equipment back to inventory.

Subtask Duration

2 days

A WBS shows the scope of project work. You use it to develop estimates, assign personnel to tasks, and track progress. The underlying idea is to subdivide each complex activity into the smallest units possible to make the work more manageable.

It isn't hard to create a WBS. You just:

- Ask what must be done to accomplish each major task in the project.

- Keep asking this question until you've broken everything down into components or tasks that you don't want to subdivide further.

- Estimate how long it will take to complete each of these smaller tasks and how much each will cost in dollars and person-hours.

As a rule, you'll stop subdividing tasks when you reach the point where the work will take the smallest unit of time you want to schedule. If you want to schedule to the nearest day, for instance, break down the work into tasks that take at least a day to perform. A WBS typically consists of three to six levels of subdivided activities. The more complex the project, the more levels it will have. Generally speaking, no project should have more than 20 levels—and only an enormous project would have that many.

Estimating the duration of a task isn't always simple or straightforward, but you'll get better at it as you gain experience. In the meantime, base your estimates on the average expected time to perform a task, not on hopes or prayers. Don't allow them to become firm commitments at this stage. When you talk to stakeholders about your estimates, share all the assumptions and risks that you've built into them.

Here in the planning phase, don't worry too much about the sequence of activities. You'll take care of scheduling later, in the build-up phase. For now, use the WBS to create the framework you'll fill in once you have a better sense of your staff, budget, and time constraints.

Padding your estimates is sometimes an acceptable way to reduce risk. If you take that route, however, do it openly and tell your stakeholders why. For example, you may base an estimate on receiving certain products within a two-week window. Make that expectation clear. Explain what the costs of a late arrival would be, and add those to your estimate if you think it's a likely risk.

Thoughtful planning yields a rough estimate of how many people and what skills you'll need. You'll also have a good idea of how long the project will take. The plan is the foundation for the build-up phase, which we'll cover next.

Building Up
Your Project

Building Up Your Project

With your plan in place, it's time to get the project under way. In the build-up phase, you'll follow these steps:

1. Assemble your team.

2. Set the schedule.

3. Develop a budget.

As in the previous chapter, we'll explore each step individually.

Assemble your team

Now that you've used the Work Breakdown Structure to estimate the required activities and tasks, you can begin recruiting people who have the skills you need.

Since you want a phenomenal team, not an ordinary one, try hard to get the best people you can. If you can't find them in your own organization, investigate the possibility of bringing them in from somewhere else. It's often more productive to import a great team member from another department (or even outside the company) than to rely on a mediocre contributor from the next cubicle.

Of course, project managers don't always get to choose their people. If your team has been assigned to you, you will need to assess members' skills and compare them with the skills you need for the project. You may decide to provide training or hire an outside expert to fill some gaps. If so, factor the additional money and time into your budget and schedule.

---

*Picking a good team is about picking
qualified people who like working in a group.
And I like giving people chances, breaking them
into new jobs. I see the potential in the people
and help them move up the ladder. A lot of people
in my position see the potential but they don't
want to take the risk. But I'm willing to.*

—**Jennifer Sargent, film and video producer**

Companies often create cross-functional teams, which consist of individuals from different departments or organizations. Leading a group like that can be tough, especially when members haven't worked together before. As the project manager, you're responsible for integrating their efforts. But your team members must understand how to manage their own parts of the project, and they must all be willing to work as a group.

HERDING CATS

How hard can it be to lead a project team? Consider the following fictional but all-too-common scenario:

When Brett first launched the PR campaign for his company's new product line, he loved the creative energy in the air. But now, a month into the project, that electricity has turned to static. Kelly and Joe are designing speeches and press briefings that don't seem to fit together. They keep asking Brett for lists of speakers. When he says they should line up the speakers themselves, they complain that they have too much other work to do. Meanwhile, the marketing people are demanding information that Brett doesn't have. Worst of all, his boss just asked if the division head could visit and get a progress update. How far along is his team? When will the company begin to see results?

_____

Brett doesn't know. He's in charge, so he's clearly doing something wrong—but what? How can he get the project back on track before someone pulls the plug on it?

Brett probably feels that he's leading the project from hell. He'll continue to feel this way until he focuses the group on its goals and brings structure to the project. That's how he'll break the cycle of the team delegating to him.

He should meet immediately with all stakeholders—not just his boss—to check his understanding of project goals. Then he should meet with his project team to develop a concrete plan that includes milestones, key deliverables, priorities, and so on.

By revisiting the WBS—which outlines the project's scope and activities—Brett can work with his team to determine who will do what and when it will be done.

Assign people to tasks

If you've built your own team or inherited members you know, you've probably already decided who will do what. But if you're leading a new, unfamiliar group, you'll have to get to know everyone before assigning tasks. It's helpful to:

1. List the people on the project team.

2. List the required skills.

3. Talk to each team member about what skills she can contribute.

4. Match people to tasks in consultation with the group.

This method begins the process of building team communication and cohesion. Say, for instance, that the project calls for a skill no one on the team possesses. One or more team members may know someone who does have that skill. Or you can plan to have a team member trained.

Plan a kickoff meeting

Once you've assembled your team, get members involved immediately at a kickoff meeting. Go over the project's goals and plan with them in as much detail as possible. Review the proposed schedule, and discuss roles and responsibilities. Ask questions like these:

- Can everybody commit to the plan?

- Can everybody commit to the schedule?

- What is the best way for us to work together?

Encourage people to point out potential trouble spots and to offer suggestions for improvement. Take all suggestions seriously, especially in areas where the team members have more experience than you do, and adjust your estimates and activities accordingly.

TIPS FOR WORKING WITH A TEAM

- Even if you're familiar with every part of the project, chances are someone on the team will know something that you don't. Listen to those with special experience, knowledge, or skills.

- If you insist on a "my way or the highway" approach, you'll cut yourself off from important sources of wisdom, and the project will suffer. Trust your team's ability to get the job done.

- Share big-picture information with the team. If members understand the purpose of the project, they will be better able to contribute.

Set the schedule

It would be nice to be able to say, *"With the resources we have, the project will need exactly this many weeks."*

But most projects come with fixed beginning and end dates. For example, although you might like to

If they see how you're monitoring results, they'll know whether they're on track to complete the job.

- Consider delegation as a way to develop members' skills. Explain assignments clearly, and provide the resources people need to perform their tasks.

- Deflect reverse delegation. Don't feel you have to solve problems or make decisions for your team members. Instead, try to generate alternative solutions together.

get started immediately, the people or materials may not be ready for another few weeks.

Scheduling is a universal task. Every project has a schedule, and every project manager must be able to set one. And nearly everything takes longer than you think it will.

How to begin

Start by looking at a drop-dead date—one that cannot be changed. It might be the date of a trade show, for example, or a regulatory agency's deadline to receive a certain document. Whatever it is, work backward from it to set other dates. For example, if an annual report must be ready in time for the shareholders' meeting and the printer needs two weeks to produce the report, then final art and copy must go to the printer at least two weeks before the meeting. (And don't wait until the last minute to schedule your job with the printer!)

Go back to your Work Breakdown Structure, which lists the tasks that must be accomplished. Assign a deliverable to each one, such as "rough draft of survey questions" or "prototype for test marketing." You can then use these deliverables to flesh out your schedule, because you have already determined about how long each task will take. Confirm that your due dates and

TIPS FOR SCHEDULING A PROJECT

- Know which deadlines are hard and fast and which have some flexibility.

- Put a four- to six-week cap on tasks. Break down anything that's longer into smaller components.

- Don't schedule more detail than you yourself can actually oversee.

- Develop schedules according to what's logically possible. Your team can't start on task C right away if tasks A and B must be completed first.

- Record all time segments in the same increments, such as days or weeks.

- Don't create a schedule that requires your team to work overtime to meet the target dates; this doesn't leave any flexibility for handling problems that crop up later.

milestones are realistic. No project team wants to be burdened with a schedule that's impossible to meet.

At this point, it's useful to flag potential bottle-necks. These are tasks in the work flow that must be completed before other activities can begin. You may want to figure out ways to remove bottlenecks. When that's not possible, build in extra time so you can be confident they won't hold things up.

You'll need to establish a procedure for updating and revising the schedule (no schedule is permanent). Keep your stakeholders informed about any modifi-cations—and about the project's overall progress.

Using the Critical Path Method

The Critical Path Method (CPM) helps you schedule project activities and allocate resources efficiently. It shows you which tasks are **critical**—that is, which ones you absolutely must complete on schedule to fin-ish the entire project on time.

For example, consider a project involving six activities with the following requirements and time expectations:

Activity	Requirement	Time to Complete
A		5 days
B		3 days
C	A and B completed	4 days
D	B completed	7 days
E	A completed	6 days
F	C completed	4 days

You can diagram the critical path as shown in figure 2.

FIGURE 2

Critical Path Method

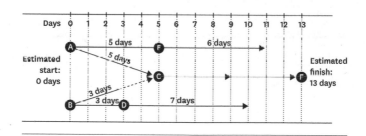

STEPS IN THE CRITICAL PATH METHOD

1. List all the activities, with brief descriptions.

2. Record how long each one will take.

3. List all tasks that must be completed before you start each activity.

4. Draw a diagram showing those task relationships.

5. Compute the earliest start time for each activity.

6. Compute the earliest finish time for each activity.

7. Identify the critical path to estimate the entire project's duration.

According to the diagram, the earliest you can complete the project is in 13 days. It also shows that activities A and E are critical to your overall deadline (you have a little wiggle room elsewhere), so you may want to devote more resources to these tasks.

Software programs can help you construct more complex versions of the critical path. But it's good to understand the basic ideas before you turn to your computer.

Gantt charts and PERT charts

There are two other widely accepted tools for scheduling and monitoring projects—bar charts such as the Gantt chart (figure 3) and flow charts such as the Performance Evaluation and Review Technique, or PERT, chart (figure 4).

A Gantt chart illustrates the status of your project, its estimated duration, the duration of each task, and the sequence of activities. Using project management

FIGURE 3

Gantt chart

Activities	4/8–4/14	4/15–4/21	4/22–4/28	4/29–5/5	5/6–5/12	5/13–5/19	5/20–5/26
Install new servers	▓						
Obtain equipment		▓					
Implement equipment			▓				
Test equipment			▓				
Go live with new equipment				▓	▓		
Repeat testing				▓	▓	▓	
Decommission old equipment						▓	
Evaluate process							▓

FIGURE 4

PERT chart

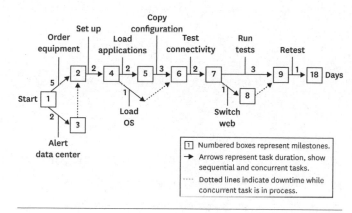

☐	Numbered boxes represent milestones.
→	Arrows represent task duration, show sequential and concurrent tasks.
····	Dotted lines indicate downtime while concurrent task is in process.

software, you can easily build one that shows which tasks must be completed before another begins.

Some project managers prefer PERT charts. Because it illustrates the critical path and lays out project milestones, a PERT chart is a handy tool for communicating the big picture to team members. It shows the following:

- When every project task within a phase should begin.

- How much time is scheduled for each task.

- All tasks in progress at a given time.

- All the dependencies between outcomes, tasks, and events.

Again, you can easily build one with software. As you track your project's progress, however, you may need to revise the chart. For example, if the time between dependent tasks exceeds your estimates, you'll have to make up for that elsewhere in the schedule to meet your deadline.

Choosing your scheduling system

In all likelihood, you'll wind up using bar charts and flow charts at different times. Both scheduling methods help you visualize what has to be done, how long a particular activity will take, what order the tasks must follow, and who is responsible for each.

Bar charts are good for showing stakeholders and end users how the project is progressing. A flow chart may be better for managing tasks and communicating detailed information to supervisors and the people doing the work. It's an especially powerful tool in networked computer environments where everyone can track the group's progress in real time.

The best method for scheduling a project, of course, is the one that you're most comfortable with and that works best for the task at hand. Think about how you track your own work and determine how satisfied you are with that approach. That may help you decide whether to stay with your current system or try a new one.

Using software for project scheduling

Most project managers use software programs to help with project scheduling and management. To determine which one is best for you, research the various options online. Get recommendations from other people, and compare their work habits and projects with your own to decide whether the software is likely to be a good fit. Unless you're already familiar with the software, make sure you can get reliable training and technical support for it. (See sidebar, "Tips on Selecting Project-Management Software.")

And remember—software is not infallible. It can't compensate for faulty logic in assembling a schedule, and it can't predict all the risks involved. Review the schedule carefully with another team member or stakeholder before finalizing it.

Develop a budget

The budget is the project's financial blueprint. It translates activities into money, showing what you have to spend and (often) what you expect your

TIPS ON SELECTING
PROJECT-MANAGEMENT SOFTWARE

Any software you choose should:

- Produce detailed schedules and budgets.

- Create bar charts and flow charts, such as Gantt and PERT charts, and calculate critical paths.

- Allow you to change the information in the charts easily.

- Integrate project schedules with a calendar allowing for weekends and holidays.

- Let you create different scenarios for contingency planning and updating.

- Alert you when you're overscheduling individuals or groups.

returns to be. Most project managers have some lee-way in their budgets. But in some contexts (such as grant-sponsored nonprofits), the budget is a contract, and money allocated for one line item cannot be spent on another line item without preapproval.

Begin developing your budget by determining the project's costs. You can usually break them down into the following categories:

- *Personnel.* This is typically the largest part of your budget. Have you included both the costs of your current team members and any contract workers you may need to add?

- *Travel.* Is everyone on site, or will you bring in people from other locations?

- *Training.* Does everyone know how to use the equipment or tools needed to accomplish the work? Do your team members possess all the required skills? If they require training, can it take place on-site, or will it involve travel?

- *Supplies.* Will you need any specialized materials or equipment in addition to the usual range of office supplies and tools?

- *Space.* Will you have to relocate people to do the work? How much room will they require, and at what cost?

- *Research.* Will you have to buy studies or data to support this project? Will you need outside research help?

- *Capital expenditures.* Will you require any capital equipment—machinery, specialized computer equipment, and so on—to do the job?

- *Overhead.* What is your projected overhead expense? (Keep it in line with your company's standard overhead percentage.)

Once you've entered the figures from these standard categories into the budget, ask yourself what you forgot. For example, did you overlook training costs at the back end to teach users to implement your project? What about additional insurance premiums, licensing fees, or costs for support or maintenance?

A budget, no matter how carefully planned, is just your best guess. Track your actual expenditures carefully—they'll probably deviate from your original estimates. Unless you're tied into specific amounts for specific line items, stay as flexible as possible within your overall budget.

Managing Your Project

Managing Your Project

In the implementation phase, where you're managing and monitoring your project against the plans and preparations you've made, you have to maintain a positive attitude to keep your team motivated. You also need to watch carefully for barriers, bottlenecks, and foul-ups. It can be a tough balancing act. You and your team will see progress in this phase—the work is actually being done. But the details can at times feel tedious, even overwhelming, and potential pitfalls are always lurking around the corner.

Let's look at some ways to maximize the progress and ease the stress.

If you thought you could plan for everything, you should probably be locked up. You have to be aware, attuned to what's happening, what's changing—and part of that is being obsessive, being on top of the details. You have to be aware of change so you can utilize whatever it is that just changed, because it might be an opportunity. And you have to monitor change so you can avoid risk downstream.

—Timothy O'Meara, director, telecommunications company

Delegate—but track results

In the planning phase, you assembled your team and assigned responsibilities to each member. But as you implement your plans, you may find that you need to delegate more tasks than you originally an-ticipated. Be flexible enough to make adjustments as you go.

Deciding what to delegate

You'll delegate two kinds of tasks. The first consists of routine activities that pretty much anyone on the team can do. With these, you want to ensure that everyone shoulders a fair portion and no one is saddled with all the mundane work.

What's the second kind? Tasks that require special-ized skills. If any of your team members possess these skills, you can delegate such activities to them. If not, you may need to hire outside experts.

As project manager, you're responsible for the overall project. So don't delegate tasks that only you can perform, such as monitoring the budget.

Trust and track

Managers used to monitor their subordinates closely, telling them what to do every step of the way. The system was called "command and control."

Most companies these days have given up that kind of management for something more like "trust and track." You assign tasks to team members, and you make sure everyone has the skills, information, and resources they need to succeed. Then you back off and let them do their jobs. But you ask for regular (short) reports on what they've done, and you monitor their progress against the schedule and budget, as described in the following sections.

Monitor progress against the schedule

Whether you do it by hand or use project management software, you need a systematic method of checking

off tasks as people complete them. No single monitoring system works for all projects. One that's right
for a large project can easily swamp a small one with
unnecessary complexity. And a system that works for
small projects won't have enough muscle for a big one.

Most project managers use software for everything
except very small undertakings. But which program is
best—and which features you need—depends on the
size and scope of your project. Do some research and
make inquiries before you decide what to use and how
to use it.

Focus on what's important

As you track the details of a project, it's easy to get
lost in the weeds. Keep asking yourself the following
questions to maintain a big-picture view:

- What do we need to accomplish with this
  project?

- What activities are essential to its overall success?

- Which elements are the most important to monitor?

- Where are the major bottlenecks?

- Where must we place controls to keep things on track?

Emphasize timely information

To respond usefully when problems or unexpected events crop up, you need to receive quick, frequent progress reports. Ideally, you'll be updated in real time so you always know exactly where the project stands. In many cases, however, you'll have to rely on weekly updates. Just be sure those come in on time and accurately reflect the status of each task.

Be prepared to take corrective action when something goes off the rails; otherwise, all you're doing is monitoring, not exercising control. But don't jump in too quickly. Allow your team members to work out most problems on their own.

Every project has milestones along the critical path. Milestones are, simply put, the points at which something should have been accomplished, with dire consequences if it hasn't been. The responsibility for meeting milestones may be someone else's, but the failure to meet them reflects badly on you and your team. As project manager, you are accountable for failures in a project even if you didn't cause them.

—Martin Nemzow, high-tech consultant

Monitor progress against the budget

One of your most important responsibilities is tracking the budget. Regardless of how carefully you have planned, actual costs rarely match what you have budgeted. Good project managers maintain the original estimates as a reference point, but they also keep a running tally of where they have run over or under budget. If they see that the total budget is likely to exceed the original amount, they make their case as soon as possible to whoever holds the purse strings—with a clear explanation as to why they'll need more money.

When monitoring actual costs, watch out for these common contingencies, which can upset your original estimates:

- Unanticipated price hikes from suppliers and subcontractors

- Estimates based on different costing methods—for example, hours versus dollars

- Unplanned personnel costs required to keep the project on schedule, including increased overtime

- Unexpected space needs

- Unexpected training costs

- Consultant fees to resolve unforeseen problems

As real expenses start rolling in, watch for significant deviations from budgeted amounts. Then find out the reason for the differences.

Not all budget news is bad. When you monitor your budget against real costs, you may find that you are actually spending less than expected. Everybody likes to hear that kind of news, as long as the agreed-upon work is being performed to the appropriate quality standards.

Ensure quality control

Quality assurance will play a major role in the success of your project. The last thing you need is a client, customer, supervisor, or other stakeholder who is dissatisfied with the end result. How to ensure quality? A few guidelines will help:

- Determine quality benchmarks in the planning phase. Consider the quality policy of the organization, stakeholder requirements, the scope of the project, and any external regulations or rules.

- Don't rush quality checks to meet deadlines. The cost of fixing problems after the fact is usually far greater than the cost of confronting and solving problems early on.

- Examine deliverables using the most appropriate tools—for example, detailed inspections, checklists, or statistical sampling.

- Accept or reject deliverables based on previously defined measures. Rejected deliverables can be returned or reworked, depending on costs.

Report progress to stakeholders

Back in the planning phase, you agreed with your stakeholders how and when you'd present your updates. As the project progresses, consult with them to make sure you're giving them the right amount of information in a useful format. Your journey to completion will be smoother without unhappy stakeholders demanding more or different information. Try using a guide, such as the one shown in figure 5.

If you hide or downplay problems as they come up, they may grow into full-blown crises, becoming twice as big as they would have if you'd alerted your stakeholders early on. So be honest with them at every step. They may even turn out to be useful resources, offering help to fix the problems.

FIGURE 5

Project management tools

Project Progress Report

Use this form to help assess progress, present this information to others, and think through next steps.

Project: **Prepared by:**

For the period from: to:

CURRENT STATUS

Key milestones for this period:

Achieved	Coming up next

Key issues or problems:

Resolved	Need to be resolved

Key decisions:

Made	Need to be made	By whom	When

Budget status:

IMPLICATIONS

Changes in objectives, time line/delivery dates, project scope, resource allocation (including people and financial):

NEXT STEPS

List the specific action steps that will be done to help move this project forward successfully.
Put a name and date next to each step if possible.

Step	Person responsible	Date

Comments

Dealing with Your Project's Problems

Dealing with Your Project's Problems

Managing projects often means dealing with the unexpected, which can be both exciting and nerve-racking. You'll face problems that you aren't sure how to handle—and sometimes these can threaten the project's success.

Scope creep

One of the most common issues is scope creep. Your client or some group of stakeholders wants you to add new deliverables to the project. (In software circles, this phenomenon is sometimes called "feature creep.")

This is only human: once people see that you can probably accomplish A, B, and C, they begin thinking that D and E might be good as well. It's why some homeowners set out to replace a sink and a countertop and end up remodeling their kitchens.

As project manager, you have an obligation to consider reasonable changes in scope. However, you also must remind stakeholders that they can't increase scope without also increasing the budget, adding time, or both. Unless those changes can be made to the satisfaction of all concerned, it's your job to stick to the project's original scope.

Delays

It's also common to fall behind schedule. Some delays are unavoidable, but often you can remedy or improve the situation. The first step is to recognize the problem. If you've been monitoring progress carefully, you'll quickly notice when schedules are readjusted

TIPS FOR CONTROLLING PROJECT SLOWDOWNS

Try these approaches before assuming you'll miss the project deadline:

- Reexamine budgets and schedules to see if you can make up the time elsewhere.

- Determine whether you can drop any elements or features.

- Deploy more resources—but weigh the additional costs against the importance of the deadline.

(continued)

---

to accommodate delays or unexpected bottlenecks. The second step is to address the situation with your team. Team members may have ideas about how to get around the problem or compensate for it by implementing other parts of the project faster than planned.

- Substitute a readily available item or seek alternative sources for whatever is causing the bottleneck.

- Offer bonuses or other incentives for on-time delivery.

- Demand better compliance. (This may require support from upper management.)

- Renegotiate with stakeholders to increase the budget or extend the deadline.

Budget overruns

Cost overruns happen all the time, but that doesn't make them any easier to deal with. When you notice that costs are creeping upward beyond what you have budgeted, you really have only three choices.

- Identify ways to reduce other expenses in those line items. If the hours for task #1 are exceeding your budget, maybe you can get task #2 or #6 done faster and more cheaply than planned.

- Find savings elsewhere in the budget. Look at every line item to see whether you can reduce expenditures below budgeted levels.

- Inform your stakeholders or client of the cost overruns in hopes of getting more resources allotted to the project. If you choose this route, be aware that it will be difficult—and that you'd better have a good explanation for why your costs are exceeding budget.

One important rule always applies: small cost overruns are easier to handle than big ones. If you stay on top of your expenditures week in and week out, you'll be better able to address overruns before they spiral out of control.

People issues

People problems are often the most difficult challenges in project management. Rather than ignoring, denying, or avoiding them, address them quickly and decisively. The list of problems in figure 6 will help you recognize and deal with some of the different situations you'll encounter.

Try to handle people problems before they get too big. Pay attention to small signs, such as a team member's increased irritability, loss of enthusiasm, or difficulty making decisions. Communicate with your team as frequently as you can, particularly when you sense trouble. Weekly staff meetings may not be enough; daily communication—with individuals and with the team as a whole—may be necessary.

FIGURE 6

Team structure problems

Problem	Possible causes	Potential impact	Recommended action
Your team lacks necessary skills.	• You over-looked certain skill require-ments during planning. • You discovered a need for new skills in the midst of the project.	• The project doesn't move forward as fast as it should, or it stalls.	• Arrange for a team member to be trained in the skills needed. • Hire outside consultants or contractors who have the skills.

Problem	Possible causes	Potential impact	Recommended action

A team member leaves.	• This could happen for many reasons, ranging from sudden illness to departure from the organization.	• Severity depends on the skills and knowledge lost:
		  – If you can easily redis-tribute the work or hire someone with the same ex-pertise, the impact may be slight.
		  – If not, the loss could create a crisis.
			• Have backup team members at the ready.
			• Cross-train people so they can fill in for one another.
			• Make one person's departure an opportunity to bring an even more skilled team member on board.

(continued)

Interpersonal problems

Problem	Possible causes	Potential impact	Recommended action
Team members are *too* friendly.	• They spend excessive amounts of time chatting or discussing personal problems.	• Overall productivity decreases. • Time is wasted, and the project slows down. • Hard-working team members resent those who work less efficiently.	• Emphasize that social gatherings need to be planned for after work. • Reorganize team subgroups to disrupt cliques.

Problem	Possible causes	Potential impact	Recommended action
Conflicts exist within the team.	• People have a hard time reconciling different personalities, working styles, or areas of expertise.	• The schedule, quality of work, overall productivity, and team cohesiveness could all suffer.	• Focus team members on the project's goals, not on personal feelings. • Separate the underlying causes from the surface disturbances, so you can solve problems at the root. • Propose solutions, not blame.

Productivity problems

Problem	Possible causes	Potential impact	Recommended action
Time is spent on the wrong tasks.	• People manage their time poorly. • A team member prefers some tasks over others, regardless of relative importance. • You've sent the wrong message about priorities.	• Work on critical tasks is delayed. • The overall project is delayed.	• Clarify which tasks are most important. • Assign tasks to pairs of team members to work on together so they can keep each other in check. • Provide resources to help members improve time management skills.
Problem	Possible causes	Potential impact	Recommended action
The quality of the work is poor.	• A team member misunderstands the requirements of the job. • Different people measure the work by different standards. • Someone doesn't have adequate skills to complete a task.	• Work must be redone, costing money and time. • The project falls.	• Be clear from the start about quality expectations and standards of measure. • Develop an action plan for improving the quality of the team member's work. • Provide training and support to develop skills.

WHAT ABOUT THE THINGS YOU CAN'T CONTROL?

Here's a nightmare scenario for any project manager (fortunately, it's fictional):

Last year, the holiday season was not a happy one for Randy. When Bright Light, Inc., failed to deliver a key part, the whole Tyranna-Bot project had come to a grinding halt. The only Tyranna-Bots to hit the market in time had been drawn from existing stock. This year, Randy found a more reliable vendor and built extra time into the schedule, yet here he was, facing another disaster. The chips that made Megala-Bot talk were defective. The supplier was scrambling for more, but there would be another serious delay, and the extra time in the schedule wouldn't cover it. Randy didn't want to stop the project, as he had last time, but how could he keep the job on schedule? The advertising blitz was under way and customers were waiting for their Megala-Bots. Randy did not want to disappoint them—or his boss.

What to do? Randy has to begin thinking of ways around the bottleneck. That probably means scouting for other vendors, paying more for extra production runs, and lining up last-minute distribution channels. He also needs to review his critical path to determine whether any adjustments in sequence can be made; for example, can packaging be prepared prior to the receipt of the finished product rather than waiting until after delivery?

Bringing Your Project to a Successful Conclusion

Bringing Your Project to a Successful Conclusion

The final stage in the life cycle of a project is the phaseout, during which your team completes its work. If all went as planned—the tasks fulfilled, the problems solved, the stakeholders satisfied—then congratulate yourself and your team. It's a time for celebration.

If, as is more likely, you hit some rough spots along the way—the project took longer than expected, the result was less than hoped for, or costs exceeded estimates—it's still important to recognize the team's efforts and accomplishments.

In either case, before the team moves on to other projects or breaks up and parts company, debrief and document the process together so that the full benefit of lessons learned can be shared.

Prepare the handoff

Some projects—a book, a house, a software program —are products, delivered to the client complete. They may need some final tweaking, but once they are done they are done, and the project manager's responsibility comes to an end.

Other projects, such as a new call-center protocol or a new procedure for hospital intake, may not have such neat-and-clean endings. The project team develops the process, modifies it as necessary, and hands it off to operating managers on the go-live date. In principle, the operating managers are responsible for it from then on. In practice, project team members may be called in to consult and to adjust the process as necessary.

Especially in the latter case, it's the project manager's job to prepare the client to assume responsibility. *Here is what we agreed the new process will accomplish. Here's what we came up with, and here's what you'll need to do to carry it out.* The transition from project to regular operations is often difficult, but you can't avoid it—and it's often the key to success.

Conduct a post-project evaluation

In a post-project evaluation, you bring your team together for one last meeting to identify what went well and what went wrong. Make a list of best practices and lessons learned to help future projects go more smoothly. Discuss how to improve the process and avoid problems during the next project.

Encourage a spirit of learning. Use the evaluation as an opportunity to figure things out, not as a time to criticize and blame. If some team members fear they'll be punished for past problems, they may try to hide those problems rather than think about better ways of handling them in the future.

If possible, bring in an outside facilitator. An outsider can objectively assess the information presented and set a constructive tone for the team's discussions. Team members often lose perspective after working so closely with one another. A skilled facilitator can sort out the emotional issues from the practical ones.

Develop a useful final report

The final report documents all the information that will be useful not only for the current project manager, team members, and stakeholders, but also for people planning future projects.

A typical post-project evaluation report includes the following:

- *Project status.* What were the original objectives, and what was achieved?

- *Future status.* Was the project a self-contained entity that has now completed its goals? Or will it be incorporated into an ongoing process? If the latter, who is responsible for that process?

- *Risk assessment.* Did the project encounter any pitfalls that endangered its success? Was it in danger of running significantly over budget or incurring any other major liabilities?

- *Information relevant to other projects.* What lessons can be applied in the future?

In preparing your report, you might find the guide in figure 7 useful.

FIGURE 7

Post-evaluation report

Sample Analysis and Lessons Learned

Project name: Project Phoenix   **Date:** 5/29/20XX
Present at this session: Rafael, Phil, and Carmen

PROJECT PHASE/TASK

Equipment acquisition

What Worked

Obtained the web servers on time and on budget.

What Didn't Work

Logistical problems with availability of database servers caused a delay. Expedited order that introduced additional expense.

Ways to Improve

Need to order equipment earlier.

PROJECT PHASE/TASK

Provision and implement equipment

What Worked

Two days were recovered through the efforts of Rafael and Carmen during provisioning phase.

PROJECT PHASE/TASK

Test equipment

What Worked

Testing phase was successful; during testing, a bug in the database content was discovered and corrected prior to cutover.

PROJECT PHASE/TASK

Go live with new equipment

What Worked

Smooth cutover with minimal downtime.

What Didn't Work

Some users were unaware that there would be a brief outage.

Ways to Improve

Publicize work window to user base more aggressively.

PROJECT PHASE/TASK

Test again

What Worked

Tested fine.

(continued)

(continued)

PROJECT PHASE/TASK

Decommission old equipment

What Worked

Decommissioned sites and erased content successfully; reabsorbed stock into inventory.

What Didn't Work

Some confusion over serial numbers and inventory, but straightened out in the end.

Ways to Improve

Check serial numbers at an earlier phase to minimize problems at the end of project.

TARGET ANALYSIS

How well did the project team do...

In achieving goals and meeting project objectives?

Success: all goals were achieved.

At meeting deadlines and the final completion date?

Success: met our target date.

At monitoring and staying within budget?

Success: slight overrun was unavoidable.

TARGET ANALYSIS

How well did the project team do...

At communicating with stakeholders?

Partial success: we could have done better at communicating requirements earlier to individuals involved in the phases of the project.

RESOURCES ASSESSMENT

Were the allocated resources appropriate, sufficient, and efficiently used? (i.e., time, people, money)

Generally, the resource allocations were appropriate. The project went slightly over budget, but was not inappropriate. The people involved had the expertise necessary to carry out the highly technical phases of the project. The time resources were appropriate, as the project was completed on time with no room to spare.

LESSONS LEARNED

What are the key lessons learned that can be applied to future projects?

At each phase of the project, it is crucial to anticipate the next steps and to alert groups or individuals of resource requirements as early as possible in the process. By so doing, we probably could have acquired the equipment in a more timely manner and would not have had to scramble so much in the later phases to meet our target dates.

Thank everyone—and prepare for the next project

Sit down and thank every team member personally for his or her contribution. Acknowledge the bumps experienced in the journey, but mark the conclusion with good cheer. You may want to take everyone out for pizza or a nice dinner. This is a time for celebration and pats on the back.

Of course, you shouldn't ignore the challenges that individual team members may have presented along the way. If people were repeatedly late or uncooperative, let them know that you noticed that behavior. Help them understand that they will have a better time in the future if they can mend their ways. In your final report, make it plain that you would be glad to discuss the strengths and weaknesses of individual team members with future project leaders.

Take some time, too, for personal reflection. What were your strengths and weaknesses as a project leader? What did you learn in the course of the project, and what will you do differently next time? Project management is a skill, and like any other skill it takes a lot of practice. The more you do it, the better you will get—but only if you make a point of reflecting on your accomplishments and your setbacks.

And then? Enjoy the satisfaction of a job well done. This may be the first in a long line of successful projects.

Test Yourself

Test Yourself

Here are 10 multiple-choice questions to help you identify your baseline knowledge of project management. Answers appear at the end of the test.

1. **You've been assigned a project, and it appears to have explicit expectations and clearly outlined responsibilities. Before you begin planning, what should you do?**

   a. Ensure that the funding has been approved.

   b. Confirm that the project is solving the right problem.

2. **Why is it critical to spend time early in the planning phase identifying all the stakeholders in your project's activities or outcomes?**

    a. To find potential champions who will support the project.

    b. To ensure that the project objectives meet everyone's expectations of success.

    c. To be politically astute and identify possible obstacles early.

3. **This book advises you to beware of "scope creep." What is scope creep?**

    a. Unwittingly giving in to pressure to do more than originally planned for.

    b. Agreeing to extend the schedule without a corresponding increase in funding.

4. **When you are defining project objectives, what three variables most often determine what you can achieve?**

a. Resources, how realistic the project is, and availability of team members.

b. Complexity, time, and the expectations of stakeholders.

c. Scope, schedule, and budget.

5. **What are you doing when you create a Work Breakdown Structure?**

a. Dividing the overall project into smaller tasks and then subdividing those tasks further until you get to the desired task size.

b. Distributing the funding you have across the project objectives in order to anticipate personnel and activity costs.

6. **When assembling a team for your project, make sure you have a group that:**

a. Will get along during the project.

b. Is dedicated to the success of the project.

c. Has all the skills needed for the project.

7. You need to track what has to be done, how long each activity will take, in what order everything has to happen, and who is responsible for what. Which project management tool will do this?

   a. Work Breakdown Structure.
   b. Gantt or PERT charts.

8. Complete this statement: "A budget is not only a list of all the costs involved in executing a project but also _____."

   a. A summary of all the skills you need to complete the project.
   b. A tracking tool that allows the manager to monitor implementation.
   c. The tool that you as manager use to justify any future need for additional funds.

9. When developing budgets, project managers frequently overlook which of the following variables?

a. Personnel

b. Travel

c. Supplies

d. Maintenance

e. Research or training

10. **In the best of all possible worlds, who conducts the evaluation of a completed project?**

a. The project manager, with all stakeholders providing input.

b. An independent person who can be objective.

c. The individual(s) who identified the initial problem and project.

Answers to test questions

1: **b.** Confirm that the project will indeed meet the organization's underlying need. The expectations can be clear yet still not go to the heart of the issue. If that's the case, you run the risk of wasting time and money on a project that is headed in the wrong direction.

2: **b.** You need to know exactly what success on the project means to people or departments who will be affected by its outcomes. One of your critical tasks in the planning phase is to meld stakeholders' expectations into a coherent and manageable set of project objectives.

3: **a.** As you learn each stakeholder's definition of success, you can get caught up in trying to solve problems that are beyond the scope of your project. Don't give in to pressures to expand the project's mission unless a majority of stakeholders see that expansion as essential, and even then, be sure you are given the additional time and budget required.

4: **c.** Scope, schedule, and budget are tightly linked. You can't change one without changing at least one of the others and, potentially, the outcome of the whole project. The quality of the project's deliverables depends heavily on the available time and funding.

5: **a.** You use a Work Breakdown Structure, or WBS, to subdivide a complex activity into smaller and smaller tasks until you reach a manageable task size. This becomes the basis for developing estimates, assigning personnel, tracking progress, and showing the scope of project work.

6: **b.** Your team needs to be committed to the project. The members may not always agree, but they have to trust that they are all working toward the same goals. A team is usually assembled according to its members' skills, but having all the skills required is not necessarily the top priority when assembling a productive team. People can gain skills through training, and the team can supplement its skills with outside help when needed.

7: **b.** Both Gantt (bar) and PERT (flow) charts are generally accepted methods of scheduling projects.

Use the method that suits you and the project; there's no "right" way to schedule.

8: **b.** Experienced project managers monitor their budgets week in and week out to make sure their projects stay on track financially.

9: **d.** Maintenance is often forgotten because it's not a standard budgeting category. But once you've completed a project, you may incur ongoing costs for maintenance and support, so it's important to factor those in during budget development.

10: **b.** An outsider is usually the most objective evaluator. But if one isn't available, the project manager should do the evaluation in a spirit of learning, not with an attitude of criticism and blame.

Learn More

Introductory books

Harvard Business School Publishing. *HBR Guide to Project Management*. Boston: Harvard Business Review Press, 2013.

This practical handbook will help you: (1) build a strong, focused team, (2) break major objectives into manageable tasks, (3) create a schedule that keeps all the moving parts under control, (4) monitor progress toward your goals, (5) manage stakeholders' expectations, and (6) wrap up your project and gauge its success.

Haynes, Marion E. *Project Management. From Idea to Implementation*. Menlo Park, CA: Crisp Publications, Inc., 2009.

This step-by-step guide to project management is designed to help readers conceive, plan, implement, and evaluate any project from initial planning to finalization.

Knight, Joe, Roger Thomas, and Brad Angus, with John Case. *Project Management for Profit: A Failsafe Guide to Keeping*

Projects on Track and on Budget. Boston: Harvard Business Review Press, 2012.

    This book shows every company owner and project manager how to run projects differently. You'll benefit if you've ever: (1) been over budget on a project, (2) exceeded a time line on a project, (3) worked on a project that completely stalled as you neared the finish line, (4) lost money on a sure-thing project and had no idea why, (5) noticed that scope and feature creep held you back, (6) watched a project take three times as long as planned, (7) felt too embarrassed to perform a review of your successes and failures, (8) wondered whether your project actually made any money.

Shenhar, Aaron J., and Dov Dvir. *Reinventing Project Management: The Diamond Approach to Successful Growth and Innovation.* Boston: Harvard Business Press, 2007.

    Projects are the engines that drive innovation from idea to commercialization. But most projects fail, largely because conventional project management concepts cannot adapt to a dynamic business environment. Based on an unprecedented study of more than 600 projects in a variety of businesses and organizations worldwide, this book provides a new model for planning and managing projects to achieve superior business results.

Verzuh, Eric. *The Fast Forward MBA in Project Management*, 4th ed. New York: Wiley, 2011.

A comprehensive introduction to project management, updated to reflect changes in the business environment over the past few years. Comes with downloadable forms and spreadsheets to help you implement the techniques described. Also offers updated advice on getting the most from Microsoft Project.

Professional and reference books

Cleland, David I. *A Guide to the Project Management Body of Knowledge*, 5th ed. Newtown Square, PA: Project Management Institute, 2013.

The Project Management Body of Knowledge is an inclusive term that describes the sum of knowledge within the profession of project management. This guide provides a common lexicon for talking about project management. Includes an extensive glossary of important concepts, terms, and phrases.

Cleland, David I., and Lewis R. Ireland. *Project Management: Strategic Design and Implementation*, 5th ed. New York: McGraw-Hill Professional, 2006.

This updated classic offers guidance on applying the theory, processes, practices, and techniques of project management to support strategic planning. It includes the latest methods for using flexible teams to implement organizational strategies—especially changes to products, services, and processes.

Dinsmore, Paul C., and Jeannette Cabanis-Brewin. *The AMA Handbook of Project Management*, 3rd ed. New York: AMACOM, 2010.

This comprehensive handbook on project management is a source for project management techniques for both traditional and emerging industries. Presents critical concepts common to all projects, as well as in-depth solutions for specific areas such as change management, research and development, and international projects.

Kerzner, Harold. *Project Management: A Systems Approach to Planning, Scheduling, and Controlling*, 11th ed. New York: John Wiley, 2013.

Project management as a discipline grew out of the need during World War II for a system to manage the schedule, cost, and specifications of large multitask projects. Since that time, it has largely been employed in the construction industry. Over the past decade, however, the use of project management techniques in general business methods (planning, scheduling, and controlling) has risen sharply.

Lewis, James P. *Fundamentals of Project Management*, 4th ed. WorkSmart Series. New York: AMACOM, 2011.

Based on best practices of experts in the field, this book explains how to set up project plans, schedule work effectively, establish priorities, monitor progress, and achieve performance objectives, while working faster and more profitably.

Lewis, James P. *Project Planning, Scheduling, and Control: A Hands-On Guide to Bringing Projects in on Time and on Budget*, 5th ed. New York: McGraw-Hill, 2010.

This application-oriented guide can be used to manage many different types of projects. Topics addressed include: how to decide if project management is needed; setting up the seven components of a project management system; applying the method of paired comparison to establish priorities and objectives; the eight areas for planning; and the project manager's role.

Articles

Barrows Jr., Edward A., and Andy Neely. "Managing Projects in Turbulent Times." *Balanced Scorecard Report*. January 2012 (product #B1201D).

Many initiatives suffer from poor project management: They are launched without clear business cases, paid too little attention by senior leaders, and managed without strong project governance. The costs of these and other mistakes are significant. The authors of this article describe four practices organizations can implement right away to improve their project management and their overall execution of strategy.

Johnson, Lauren Keller. "Close the Gap Between Projects and Strategy." *Harvard Management Update*. June 2004 (product #U04060).

Companies must rein in and give focus to their ever more disparate arrays of projects. The key: managing projects in portfolios that both recognize the relationships between distinct projects and align them to corporate strategy.

Klein, Gary. "Performing a Project Premortem." *Harvard Business Review*. September 2007 (product #F0709A).

Projects fail at a spectacular rate. One reason is that too many people are reluctant to share their reservations during the all-important planning phase. By making it safe for dissenters who are knowledgeable about the undertaking and worried about its weaknesses to speak up, you can improve a project's chances of success.

Matta, Nadim F., and Ronald N. Ashkenas. "Why Good Projects Fail Anyway." *Harvard Business Review*. September 2003 (product #R0309H).

Big projects fail more than half the time, by some estimates. It's not hard to understand why. Complicated long-term projects are customarily developed by a series of teams working along parallel tracks. If managers fail to anticipate everything that might fall through the cracks, those tracks will not converge successfully at the end to reach the goal. To uncover unanticipated problems while the project is still in development, inject into the overall plan a series of mini-projects, or "rapid-results initiatives," that have as their goal a miniature version of the overall goal. The World Bank, for example, used rapid-results initiatives to great effect to keep a sweeping 16-year project on track and deliver visible results years ahead of schedule.

Schlesinger, Leonard A., Charles F. Kiefer, and Paul B. Brown. "New Project? Don't Analyze—Act." *Harvard Business Review*. March 2012 (product #R1203R).

How do you get a new initiative off the ground in an unpredictable environment? For insight, the authors look to experts in navigating extreme uncertainty while minimizing risk: serial entrepreneurs. These business leaders act, learn, and build their way into the future. Managers in traditional organizations can do the same, starting with smart, low-risk steps that follow simple rules: Use the means at hand; stay within an acceptable loss; secure only the commitment needed for the next step; bring along only volunteers; link the initiative to a business imperative; produce early results; and manage expectations. You gain momentum by acting on what you learn in each step.

Harvard Business School Publishing. "What You Can Learn from Professional Project Managers." *Harvard Management Update*. February 2001 (product #U0102B).

Companies that manage large capital projects or a multitude of simultaneous projects—manufacturing, engineering, and construction firms—have long recognized the need for expertise in the techniques of planning, scheduling, and controlling work. Even if you're not a certified project manager, you can benefit from the professionalization of the field.

Sources

Primary sources for this book

Harvard Business School Publishing. Harvard Manage-
Mentor. Boston: Harvard Business Publishing, 2002.

Harvard Business School Publishing. *HBR Guide to Project
Management*. Boston: Harvard Business Review Press,
2012.

Harvard Business School Publishing. *Pocket Mentor: Managing Projects*. Boston: Harvard Business School Press,
2006.

Index

Notes

Notes